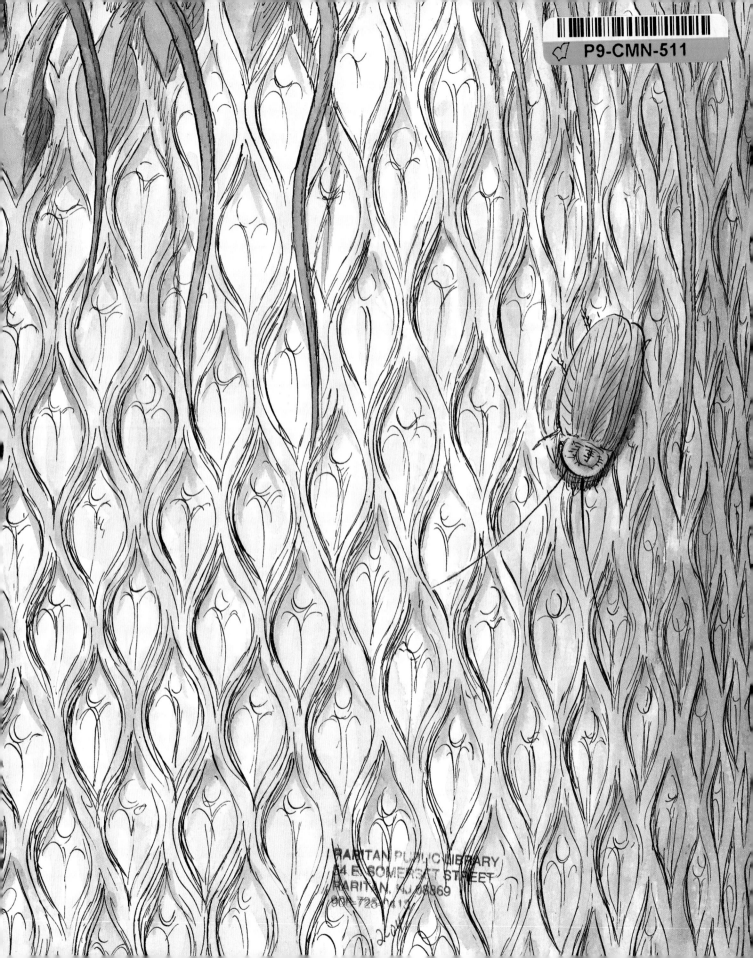

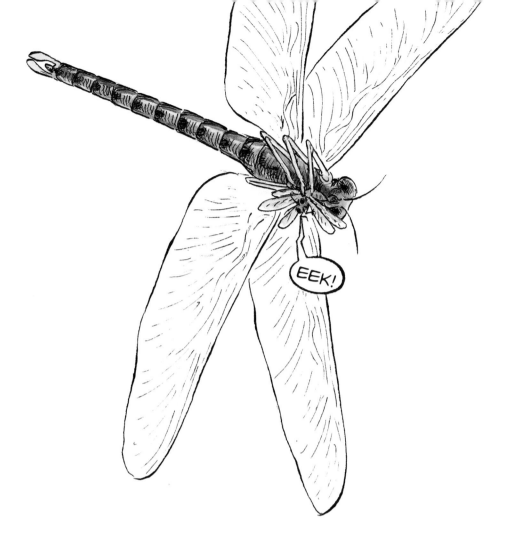

For my parents, Tony and Eve

When Bugs Were Big, Plants Were Strange, and Tetrapods Stalked the Earth

A Cartoon Prehistory of Life Before Dinosaurs

WRITTEN AND ILLUSTRATED BY

HANNAH BONNER

NATIONAL GEOGRAPHIC

WASHINGTON, D.C.

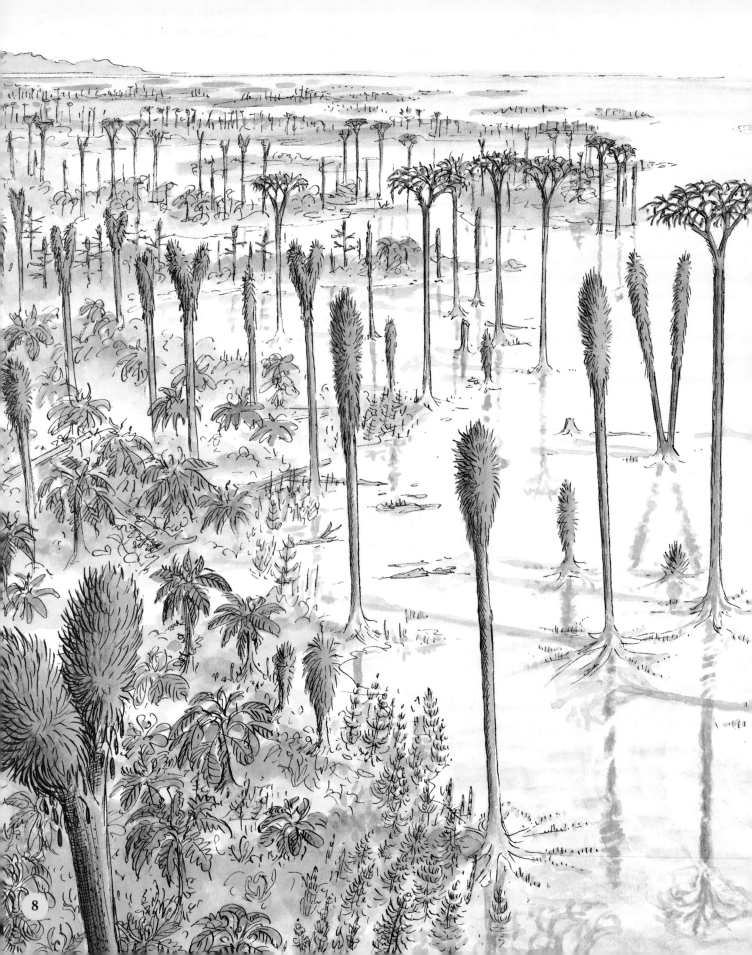

WELCOME TO THE
COAL SWAMPS

Mid-afternoon, 320 million years ago. It rained this morning, but now the sun is out and steam is rising from the coal swamps. Rivers meander out toward the sea through huge marshy deltas that are covered in strange forests.

It's very quiet except for some buzzing insects and the sound of water rippling as an amphibian swims by.

TODAY WILL BE HOT AND MUGGY, JUST LIKE EVERY OTHER DAY FOR THE NEXT SEVERAL MILLION YEARS! SHOWERS LIKELY.

80°

92°

93°

86°

Let's take a look at the plants that grew in the swamps back then. The tall trees belong to an ancient group called lycopods. Their young looked like hairy telephone poles, the full-grown ones like something out of a Dr. Seuss book.

The only lycopods still alive today are club mosses and their relatives, puny little plants you might find on the forest floor. Ancient lycopod trees came in a variety of shapes. Scientists have given them long Latin names.

DIAPHORODENDRON   PARALYCOPODITES   SIGILLARIA.

One of the strangest things about these trees was how they grew. First the baby tree put out roots. The roots had little rootlets that could come up above the mud and photosynthesize, which means they could make their own food from sunlight. The bark on the trunks may also have been green and photosynthetic.

In a mere ten years the tree could be 90 feet (27 meters) tall. Only then did it put out branches, in order to have some place from which to dangle its cones. The cones released spores, which the wind carried away.

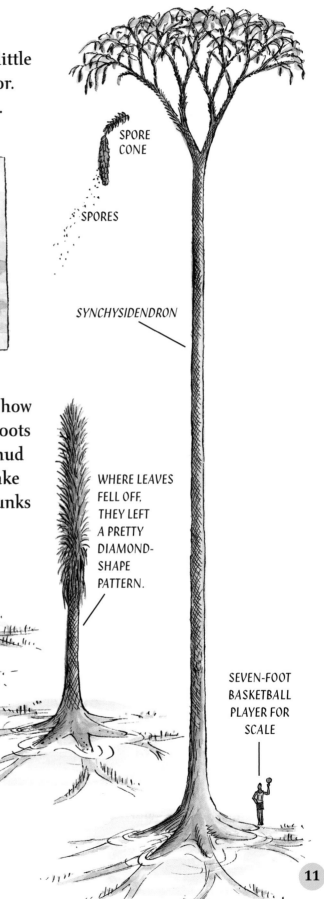

SPORE CONE

SPORES

SYNCHYSIDENDRON

WHERE LEAVES FELL OFF, THEY LEFT A PRETTY DIAMOND-SHAPE PATTERN.

SEVEN-FOOT BASKETBALL PLAYER FOR SCALE

Other plants were more familiar looking. Some of the ferns would have looked just fine in a pot in someone's living room—a waste of talent, since living rooms hadn't been invented yet. Others were tree size.

Horsetails, ferns, and lycopods all grow from spores. A spore is a tiny packet of genetic material that needs to be wet in order to turn into a new plant. The rainy, soggy swamps were a paradise for spore plants.

A TREE FERN. THERE ARE SIMILAR-LOOKING TREE FERNS ALIVE TODAY IN PLACES SUCH AS NEW GUINEA.

A SEED FERN—NOT REALLY A FERN AT ALL BUT AN EARLY SEED PLANT

CORDAITES, ANOTHER EARLY SEED PLANT

PRIMITIVE HORSETAILS. SIMILAR ONES STILL GROW IN DAMP PLACES NOWADAYS. SOME OF THE EARLY ONES FORMED BIG BUSHES AND EVEN TREES.

FOSSIL SUNSHINE

What happened to all those megatons of luxuriant, fast-growing plants when they died?

TREES FLATTENED BY A STORM.

CUTTING PEAT

In the swamps the plant matter piled up in the water and became a brown mush called peat. Peat still forms today in places called peat bogs.

Over time, the peat got buried under layers of mud and sand. The peat turned into coal, and the mud and sand turned into rock.

COAL SEAM

ROCK

This means that if your local power plant burns coal, then the electricity in your home is really solar energy captured by plants hundreds of millions of years ago through photosynthesis.

WE...AHEM!
ATTENTION PLEASE, CLASS! WE CALL THIS PERIOD THE CARBONIFEROUS BECAUSE OF ALL THE COAL IT PRODUCED.

CARBO = LATIN FOR COAL
CARBONIFEROUS PERIOD
355 - 290 MILLION YEARS AGO

THE CARBONIFEROUS PLANET

How come we find remains of tropical coal swamps in places such as Canada and Germany, which are now quite chilly? Well, during the Carboniferous period those places weren't chilly at all, and that's because of something called continental drift. Ever since they first formed, the continents have been doing the world's slowest dance, sliding around on sections of the Earth's crust called plates. Back in Carboniferous times, the continents were farther south than they are now. North America and Europe were on the Equator, where it is hottest.

IT'S NICE AND TOASTY NEAR THE EQUATOR, BUT IF YOU'RE TRAVELING SOUTH, YOU'D BETTER BRING A SCARF ALONG!

85° 87° 90° 80° 40°

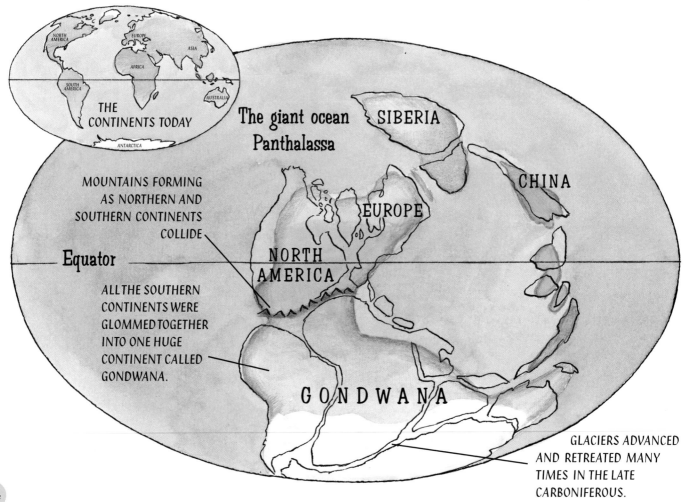

THE CONTINENTS TODAY

NORTH AMERICA
EUROPE
ASIA
AFRICA
SOUTH AMERICA
AUSTRALIA
ANTARCTICA

The giant ocean Panthalassa

SIBERIA

CHINA

MOUNTAINS FORMING AS NORTHERN AND SOUTHERN CONTINENTS COLLIDE

EUROPE

Equator

NORTH AMERICA

ALL THE SOUTHERN CONTINENTS WERE GLOMMED TOGETHER INTO ONE HUGE CONTINENT CALLED GONDWANA.

GONDWANA

GLACIERS ADVANCED AND RETREATED MANY TIMES IN THE LATE CARBONIFEROUS.

CRUNCH!

These plates apparently have no sense of direction, because they keep bumping into each other. When this happens, the land gets scrunched, and mountain ranges rise up. During the Carboniferous, the southern continent of Gondwana collided with North America and Europe and created mountains that include the Appalachians.

During the first half of the Carboniferous, shallow seas frequently flooded much of the continents.

During the second half, sea levels were lower so there was more exposed land—and many more coal swamps.

The time line on the right shows how scientists divide up the 545 million years since the beginning of the Cambrian period, when the seas were just starting to fill with animal life. This book covers the Carboniferous and Permian periods, which come at the end of the Paleozoic Era.

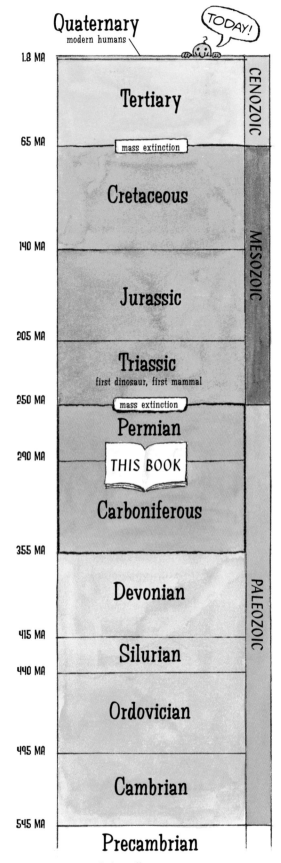

Quaternary
modern humans
TODAY!

1.8 MA

Tertiary — CENOZOIC

65 MA
mass extinction

Cretaceous

140 MA

Jurassic — MESOZOIC

205 MA

Triassic
first dinosaur, first mammal

250 MA
mass extinction

Permian

290 MA
THIS BOOK

Carboniferous

355 MA

Devonian — PALEOZOIC

415 MA

Silurian

440 MA

Ordovician

495 MA

Cambrian

545 MA

Precambrian

*MA stands for million years ago
(in Latin "million years" is "mega annum")*

BIG BUG, LITTLE BUG

Now let's get back to the swamp! Until this time, the only things crisscrossing the air had been leaves, dust, and spores carried by the wind. Now for the first time there were insects buzzing around in the humid air overhead. With bats and birds and flying reptiles still many millions of years away, these aerial pioneers could flit about at their leisure…unless a dragonfly the size of a small falcon came cruising along with an appetite!

EEK!

THE DRAGONFLY'S CARNIVOROUS NYMPH MUST HAVE BEEN EQUALLY HUGE AND THE TERROR OF LOCAL SWAMPS.

EARLY DADDY LONGLEGS

SCORPION

THE FIRST LAND SNAILS

SPIDER ANCESTOR

THERE WERE PROBABLY PLENTY OF WORMS, BUT SOFT SQUISHY THINGS RARELY GET PRESERVED AS FOSSILS.

The most common insects around were cockroaches. The leaf litter was teeming with them. Nowadays they seem especially fond of kitchens, as anyone who's gone for a midnight snack in certain New York City apartments will tell you. What makes roaches so successful that they're still all over the place today? It's probably that they're not picky eaters (they'll eat anything from rotting Carboniferous plants to wallpaper, soap, or moldy Cheerios); they like to live in warm places; and they reproduce very, very fast.

The vast majority of these insects were no bigger than their modern relatives, but many insect groups did produce at least a few XXL models. The biggest were the dragonflies, followed by mayflies and the extinct palaeodictyopterans, some of which had a 16-inch (40 centimeter) wingspan—the same as a robin's!

OHIO, 300 MILLION YEARS AGO

MANHATTAN, ZERO YEARS AGO

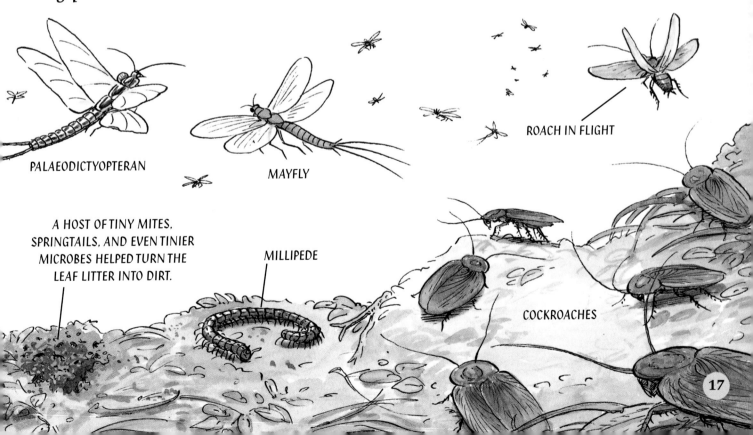

PALAEODICTYOPTERAN

MAYFLY

ROACH IN FLIGHT

A HOST OF TINY MITES, SPRINGTAILS, AND EVEN TINIER MICROBES HELPED TURN THE LEAF LITTER INTO DIRT.

MILLIPEDE

COCKROACHES

The biggest bug of all was not an insect. Imagine for a moment that you're sitting under a tree fern minding your own business, when you hear rustling noises worthy of a freight train, and along comes a 6-foot (1.8 meter) thing that looks like a huge, flattened centipede. It's called *Arthropleura*. Luckily for you, it appears to be a harmless vegetarian that uses its immensely long gut to digest plant matter, much the way cows do today.

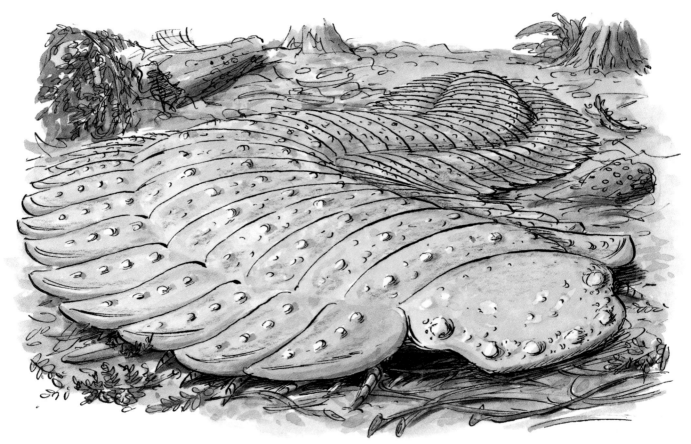

It's a pity we no longer have bugs this big…or perhaps it isn't such a pity, come to think of it! Scientists have wondered why bugs got this big only during this time. One possible explanation has to do with oxygen. There were so many plants growing then that oxygen levels in the air reached an all-time high. A bug doesn't have sophisticated lungs like ours to help it breathe, and if its body is very big it has trouble getting enough oxygen to all its different parts. The high oxygen levels allowed bigger bodies to evolve. Still, bugs didn't get big just because they could; being bigger must have had advantages, such as allowing them to get more food or have fewer enemies.

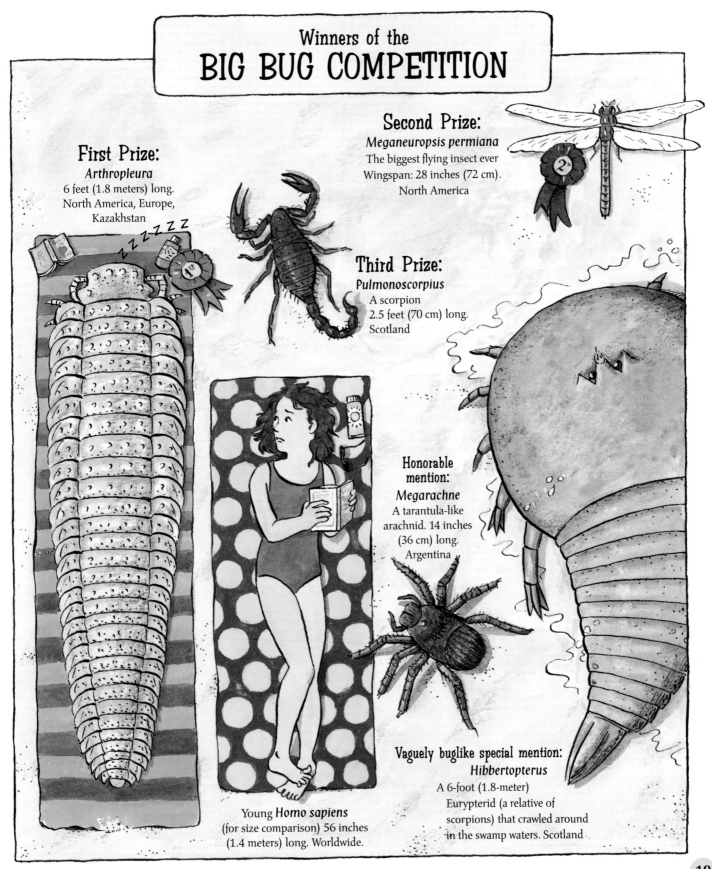

Winners of the
BIG BUG COMPETITION

Second Prize:
Meganeuropsis permiana
The biggest flying insect ever
Wingspan: 28 inches (72 cm).
North America

First Prize:
Arthropleura
6 feet (1.8 meters) long.
North America, Europe,
Kazakhstan

Third Prize:
Pulmonoscorpius
A scorpion
2.5 feet (70 cm) long.
Scotland

**Honorable
mention:**
Megarachne
A tarantula-like
arachnid. 14 inches
(36 cm) long.
Argentina

Young **Homo sapiens**
(for size comparison) 56 inches
(1.4 meters) long. Worldwide.

Vaguely buglike special mention:
Hibbertopterus
A 6-foot (1.8-meter)
Eurypterid (a relative of
scorpions) that crawled around
in the swamp waters. Scotland

19

SHARKS AND SEASHELLS BY THE SEASHORE

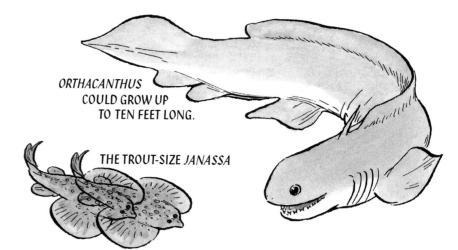

ORTHACANTHUS COULD GROW UP TO TEN FEET LONG.

THE TROUT-SIZE *JANASSA*

The waters of the swamps and of the oceans beyond were teeming with life. Fish had already been around for many millions of years and had evolved into many different models. Sharks were very common in both fresh and salt water. One of the weirdest was the 3-foot (1 meter) *Akmonistion,* which sported a mysterious "headdress" covered in spines.

THE GOLDFISH-SIZE *XENACANTHUS*

AKMONISTION

I THINK THE SHARK HID IN THE SAND, AND THE CREST SCARED OFF PREDATORS.

Scientist

I THINK IT WAS FOR MATING.

Scientist

AND I SAY TOO BAD IT'S EXTINCT 'CAUSE IT WOULD HAVE MADE A TERRIFIC CHEESE GRATER!

Chef

NOBODY KNOWS FOR SURE WHAT AKMONISTION USED ITS SPINY TURRET FOR.

In the shallow seas offshore there were reefs somewhat like our modern coral reefs, but with hardly any coral. Instead, tiny colonial animals called bryozoans, shelled creatures called brachiopods, and sponges, algae, and bivalves (clams and their relatives) all built the reef by adding their skeletons to it when they died. The same was true for crinoids and blastoids, odd things that looked like flowers but were in fact animals related to starfish and sea urchins.

SPONGE

BONY FISH

NAUTILOIDS,
RELATIVES
OF SQUID

BRYOZOANS

BRACHIOPODS

PALEOZOIC
CORALS

BIVALVES,
RELATIVES
OF CLAMS

BLASTOIDS

CRINOIDS

TRILOBITE

21

TOWERING TETRAPODS

Bugs weren't the only oversize inhabitants of the late Paleozoic. Nowadays amphibians are generally small, but prehistoric ones came in all shapes and sizes. There were big ones and little ones. Some were built to live on land, and some were swimmers. Some even lost their legs and looked like snakes.

Amphibians descended from fish in the Devonian period, and until reptiles appeared in the middle of the Carboniferous they were the only tetrapods (four-legged creatures) around.

MODERN FROG FOR SIZE COMPARISON

ERYOPS. A BIG BRUISER THAT SPENT MUCH OF ITS TIME IN THE WATER. 6.5 ft (2 m)

MOST AMPHIBIANS ATE BUGS.

SOME ALSO ATE FISH.

AND SOME, LIKE DISCOSAURISCUS, EVEN ATE THEIR OWN RELATIVES.

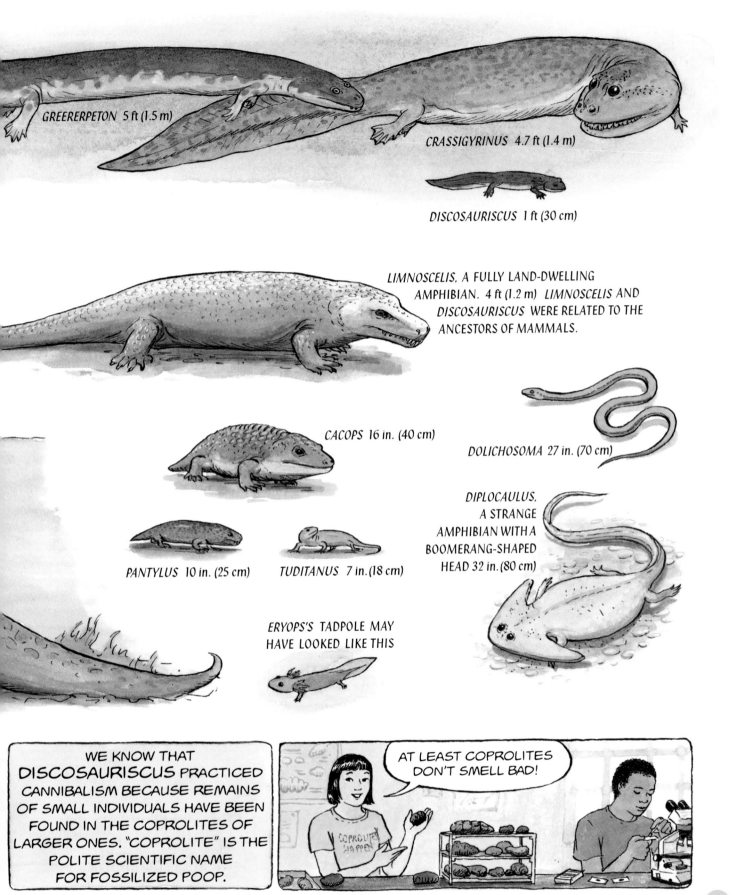

GREERERPETON 5 ft (1.5 m)

CRASSIGYRINUS 4.7 ft (1.4 m)

DISCOSAURISCUS 1 ft (30 cm)

LIMNOSCELIS, A FULLY LAND-DWELLING AMPHIBIAN. 4 ft (1.2 m) LIMNOSCELIS AND DISCOSAURISCUS WERE RELATED TO THE ANCESTORS OF MAMMALS.

CACOPS 16 in. (40 cm)

DOLICHOSOMA 27 in. (70 cm)

DIPLOCAULUS, A STRANGE AMPHIBIAN WITH A BOOMERANG-SHAPED HEAD 32 in. (80 cm)

PANTYLUS 10 in. (25 cm)

TUDITANUS 7 in. (18 cm)

ERYOPS'S TADPOLE MAY HAVE LOOKED LIKE THIS

WE KNOW THAT DISCOSAURISCUS PRACTICED CANNIBALISM BECAUSE REMAINS OF SMALL INDIVIDUALS HAVE BEEN FOUND IN THE COPROLITES OF LARGER ONES. "COPROLITE" IS THE POLITE SCIENTIFIC NAME FOR FOSSILIZED POOP.

AT LEAST COPROLITES DON'T SMELL BAD!

COPROLITES HAPPEN

Which Came First, The Chicken or the Egg?

YOU WOULDN'T BELIEVE WHAT RAISING THESE LITTLE GUYS WITHOUT A POND IS COSTING ME IN ELECTRIC BILLS, EDNA!

AN EARLY ATTEMPT AT INLAND COLONIZATION.

Like amphibians today, their prehistoric ancestors all had to lay their eggs in water. The catch: It meant they couldn't live far from a pond. In the meantime, the higher, drier areas were full of tasty bugs — and nobody to eat them. Such a waste! By the middle of the Carboniferous, some tetrapods evolved a type of egg that could be hatched on land. Instead of putting an egg in a pond, they somehow managed to put a pond in an egg: The embryo was now inside a bag of liquid called the amnion. A shell on the outside of the egg prevented it from drying out, and a big yolk fed the embryo so it could skip the tadpole stage and come out of the egg looking like a miniature copy of its parents.

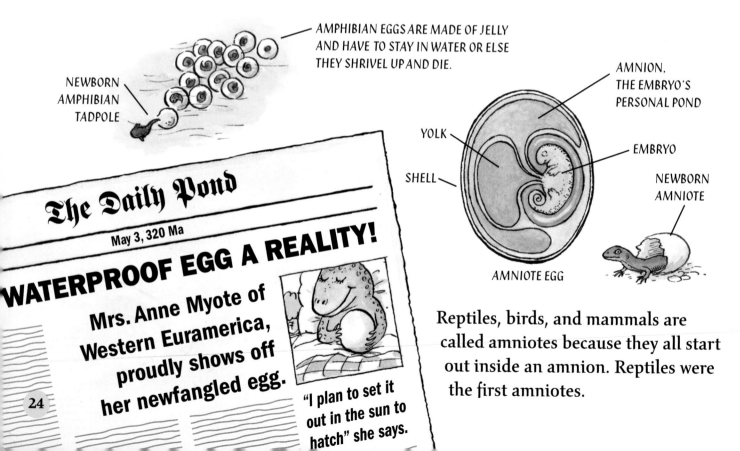

NEWBORN AMPHIBIAN TADPOLE

AMPHIBIAN EGGS ARE MADE OF JELLY AND HAVE TO STAY IN WATER OR ELSE THEY SHRIVEL UP AND DIE.

AMNION, THE EMBRYO'S PERSONAL POND

YOLK

SHELL

EMBRYO

NEWBORN AMNIOTE

AMNIOTE EGG

The Daily Pond

May 3, 320 Ma

WATERPROOF EGG A REALITY!

Mrs. Anne Myote of Western Euramerica, proudly shows off her newfangled egg.

"I plan to set it out in the sun to hatch" she says.

Reptiles, birds, and mammals are called amniotes because they all start out inside an amnion. Reptiles were the first amniotes.

FIRST AMNIOTE, 320 MILLION YEARS AGO

THEROPOD DINOSAUR, 220 MILLION YEARS AGO

ARCHEOPTERYX, 150 MILLION YEARS AGO

DOMESTIC HEN, TODAY

HASN'T ANYONE EVER ASKED YOU WHICH CAME FIRST, THE CHICKEN OR THE EGG? WELL NOW YOU KNOW!

No Paleozoic fossil eggs have been discovered so far. How, then, do paleontologists know which fossils are amniotes and which are not? They have to rely on a number of small differences in the skeleton, and they don't always agree. The oldest amniote ever found is a lizardlike reptile called *Hylonomus*. Fossils of *Hylonomus* were found inside hollow lycopod stumps in Joggins, Nova Scotia (home also to the 6-foot (1.8-meter) *Arthropleura* and other interesting animals). *Hylonomus* was a small, agile bug catcher. This was a good thing to be in a world with more and more bugs to catch.

LOOK AT THESE VERTEBRAE! IT'S AN AMNIOTE!

NO, IT'S AN AMPHIBIAN!

AMNIOTE!

AMPHIBIAN!

SIGH...

HYLONOMUS, THE WORLD'S OLDEST FOSSIL REPTILE

JOB OPPORTUNITIES

ECOLOGICAL NICHES

Position available for bug eater. Must be willing to travel far from water. Call 627-BUGS.

Bug eaters wanted for unexplored highlands. Plenty of food guaranteed. Sorry, amniotes only. Contact gus@catch.bug.

Start a new life! Seeking colonizers for the hills. Bugs-a-plenty!! No amphibians need apply. Call 800-232-7878.

All the bugs you can eat! Many perks for adventure-some egg-layers. Contact Tim@bugeaters.bug.

ECOLOGICAL NICHES

Full-time position hunti... bugs in dry areas. Send ... résumé to Reptile Reps... PO Box 432, Uplands

Are you a team player... Hungry?? Go where ... tetrapod has ever gor... before!!! E-mail to ... Bob@bugsorbu...

Bug eaters n... untravelled ... All food, ... Sorry, ar... Contac...

Star... co... E... amphi...

(partial left column)
...ing ...eaters ...lands. ...e time. ...equent. ...eat.bug

...ion hunting ...ands. Call ...ind-A-Rep, ...1, Hilltown.

Dear Mom,
The bugs here in the highlands are so juicy and plump! Wish you were here.

Liz

Mrs. Lee Zard
32 Swamp Way
Soggy Bottom

Upland Cuisine

CORDAITES, A SEED PLANT

New Frontiers

The earliest amniotes continued to hang out in the lowlands near their amphibian ancestors. Then they gradually began to head for the hills, where they colonized all sorts of new habitats. In the meantime, the climate was changing. In the late Carboniferous, the tropics began to have frequent dry spells. Most of the lovely, weird lycopod trees went extinct, and seed plants (which first appeared in the Devonian) became much more common. Seed plants were happy in this drier climate because seeds protect the plant embryo from drying out and contain lots of food to give it a good start even if conditions aren't ideal—just as amniote eggs protect and nourish animal embryos.

The Carboniferous was followed by the Permian Period. By the early Permian, seed plants had become even more common, and a whole host of amniotes had moved in among them.

EARLY CONIFERS, ANCESTORS OF OUR PINES AND FIRS

AUTUNIA, A SEED FERN

GIANT HORSETAILS, WHICH STILL GREW IN DAMP PLACES

SIGILLARIA, THE ONLY REMAINING LYCOPOD TREE

THE PERMIAN PLANET

The climate continued to get drier in the Permian. By now the continents had all come together into one supercontinent, Pangaea. This changed the pattern of ocean currents and created big inland areas, which tend to have more extreme climates. The continent had also drifted northward, bringing more of the southern landmass out of the freezer and into the temperate zone.

THE PERMIAN WAS NAMED AFTER THE RUSSIAN CITY OF PERM, WHERE THERE ARE SOME EXCELLENT ROCK LAYERS FROM THIS PERIOD.

PERMIAN
290-250 Ma

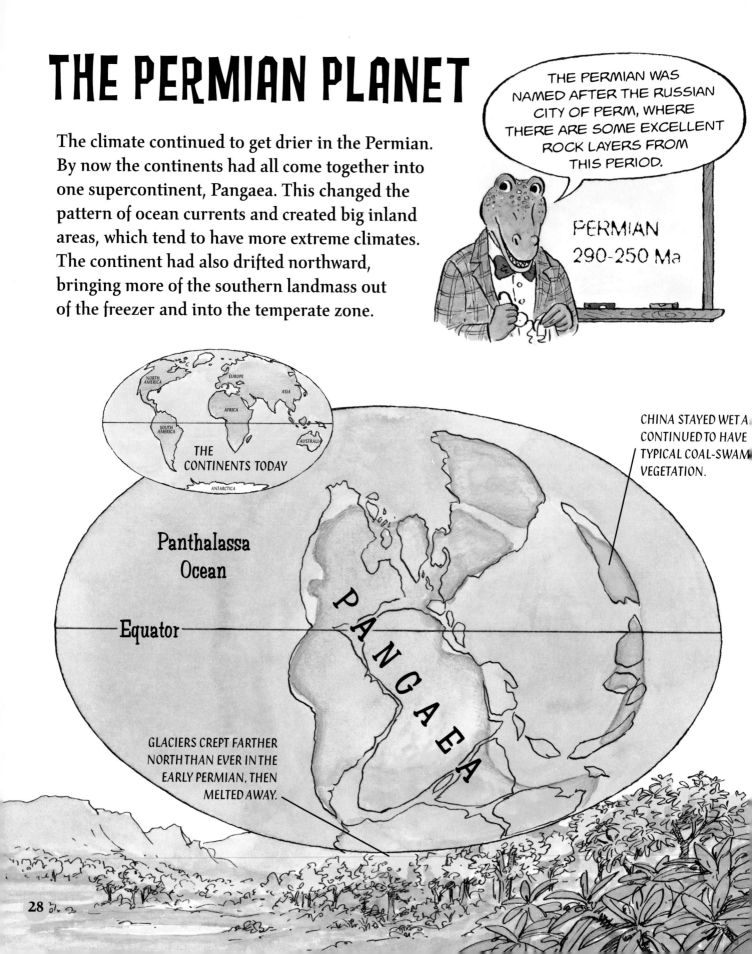

NORTH AMERICA

EUROPE

ASIA

AFRICA

SOUTH AMERICA

AUSTRALIA

THE CONTINENTS TODAY

ANTARCTICA

Panthalassa Ocean

CHINA STAYED WET A CONTINUED TO HAVE TYPICAL COAL-SWAM VEGETATION.

Equator

PANGAEA

GLACIERS CREPT FARTHER NORTH THAN EVER IN THE EARLY PERMIAN, THEN MELTED AWAY.

Many inland areas became deserts. Entire seas dried up and left behind thick crusts of salt and other minerals. These areas must have looked like the Great Salt Lake in Utah, which is suffering a similar fate.

Meanwhile the wooded parts of the Southern Hemisphere were entirely dominated by a tree called *Glossopteris.* We know that *Glossopteris* had cold winters to contend with because its wood had seasonal rings in it, and because it shed its leaves. *Glossopteris* leaves blanketed the ground every fall just as they do in our temperate forests today.

BUGS CONTINUED TO BE PLENTIFUL, AND MANY NEW INSECT FAMILIES EVOLVED.

HOT AND DRY BY DAY THIS WEEK, CHILLY AT NIGHT, NO RAIN IN SIGHT...

60°
70°
75°
60°
40°

GLOSSOPTERIS

29

REPTILES ON THE RISE

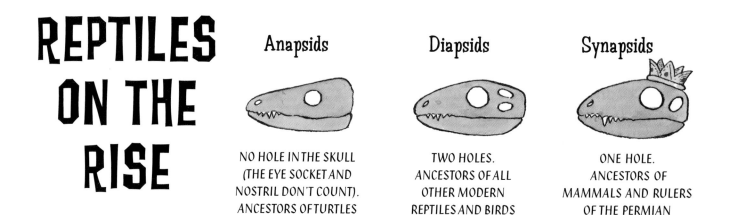

Anapsids

NO HOLE IN THE SKULL
(THE EYE SOCKET AND
NOSTRIL DON'T COUNT).
ANCESTORS OF TURTLES

Diapsids

TWO HOLES.
ANCESTORS OF ALL
OTHER MODERN
REPTILES AND BIRDS

Synapsids

ONE HOLE.
ANCESTORS OF
MAMMALS AND RULERS
OF THE PERMIAN

Now back to our story! No sooner had reptiles appeared on the scene in the middle of the Carboniferous than they began evolving along three different paths, each with a different kind of skull. Two of the groups developed holes in their skulls that allowed for new and improved jaw muscles.

WOULDN'T YOU LIKE TO BE A SYNAPSID LIKE ME?

ARE YOU KIDDING? I NEED THAT LIKE I NEED A HOLE IN THE HEAD!

Trundling Toward Turtlehood

Most anapsids were lizardlike, but one group, the pareiasaurs, produced some real hulks. One of them was *Scutosaurus*, a Permian plant-eater the size of a small cow. Today, turtles (which didn't appear until the Mesozoic) are the only living anapsids.

EOCAPTORHINUS, 1 FOOT (.3 m) LONG

SCUTOSAURUS

Lovely Lizards, Creepy Pre-Crocs

The diapsids of this period are the ancestors of all living reptiles (except for turtles). They are also the ancestors of dinosaurs, and therefore of birds as well. They started out small and lizard shaped and then branched out into two main groups.

WHAT!— THAT'S MY ANCESTOR?

PETROLACOSAURUS, THE EARLIEST DIAPSID FOUND SO FAR

The group called the archosaurs tended to be large. *Protorosaurus* was a 6-foot (1.8-meter) archosaur that may have eaten bugs or fish. *Archosaurus*, on the other hand, was a fierce meat eater with a vaguely crocodilian face. This was no coincidence, since the descendants of this group evolved into crocodiles and dinosaurs—but not until the next period, the Triassic.

ARCHOSAURUS

PROTOROSAURUS

Members of the other group, the lepidosauromorphs, kept their slim and lizardly figures and gave rise to all our modern lizards and snakes.

HOVASAURUS, A SWIMMER

PALIGUANA

COELUROSAURAVUS, A PERMIAN GLIDER

31

Meandering Toward Mammalhood

Forget anapsids and diapsids—the real rulers of the late Carboniferous and Permian periods were the ancestors of mammals, the synapsids. The first wave of them were called pelycosaurs, and they still looked decidedly reptilian. Here we see a group of pelycosaurs called *Edaphosaurus* using the tall sails on their backs as solar panels to catch the first rays of morning sun and get rid of their nighttime chill. Reptiles are sluggish when they're cold, and these plant-eaters are hoping to get up to speed before their carnivorous relative *Dimetrodon* does the same thing.

Dimetrodon had a similar sail. With the sail turned toward the sun, the blood under the surface warmed up quickly. If the animal got too hot, all it had to do was turn the sail away from the sun or stand in the shade, and its blood cooled back down.

WHOMP!

HOW UNDIGNIFIED!

THE SAILS WERE STIFF AND DIDN'T FOLD DOWN, SO THESE CREATURES MUST HAVE HAD TO BE CAREFUL NOT TO STAND SIDEWAYS TO A STRONG WIND!

DIMETRODON

OPHIACODON

HAPTODUS

VARANOSAURUS

MOST PELYCOSAURS DIDN'T HAVE SAILS.

Pelycosaurs like *Dimetrodon* and *Ophiacodon* were the fiercest carnivores the world had yet seen, preying on other large animals. Others, like *Varanosaurus* and *Haptodus*, probably ate smaller prey, including bugs. There were also large pelycosaur plant-eaters. Remember all those plant-covered uplands (and lowlands)? They provided a nonstop veggie buffet for these vegetarians, and no one was more into it than a group called the caseids. The caseids became big blob-shaped eating machines. To judge by their huge waistlines and tiny heads, they must have been both slow and dim-witted, which makes one wonder how they managed not to get eaten. Maybe they were too big to bother with, or maybe they tasted really, really bad—there is much fossil bones will never tell us.

COTYLORHYNCHUS, A LARGE CASEID

CASEIDS AT THE DINER

WOULD YOU FOLKS LIKE SEED-FERN OR REGULAR?

DUH?

DUH?

ARE THESE GUYS DUMB, OR WHAT?

I'LL JUST BRING REGULAR, HOW ABOUT THAT?

A ll good things must come to an end, and eventually a new group of carnivorous synapsids emerged called the therapsids. Apparently the first thing on their "to do" list was either to out-compete the pelycosaurs or have them for lunch. After eating the last of the synapsid plant eaters, some of the therapsids themselves became vegetarians, and the first large land animal food chain was born: Lots of herbivores turning plants into meat, and a smaller number of carnivores preying on them.

The most common herbivores by far were porky little guys called dicynodonts. They had a horny beak instead of front teeth, and some of them lived in burrows in the ground, woodchuck-style. There were also big, lumbering plant eaters like *Moschops*. *Moschops* had a thick, rocklike skull. Scientists think it was the world's first head-butter. Since head-butting is usually done by social animals to establish who's boss, it may mean that *Moschops* lived in herds the way modern bison do.

MOSCHOPS

DIICTODON,
A DICYNODONT

34

The carnivorous therapsids in the meantime were becoming more and more mammal-like. Dog-size *Lycaenops* was one example. It stood higher off the ground than earlier synapsids (which helped it run better), and looked like what you would get if you crossed a lizard with a German shepherd.

LYCAENOPS

Even more mammal-like was *Procynosuchus*. *Procynosuchus* showed signs of a faster, warmer metabolism. For one thing, it could breathe and chew at the same time, thanks to a shelf separating the inside of its nose from its mouth. This was important because as a more active, warm-blooded animal, it needed to chop up its food so it could digest it more quickly. Reptiles, on the other hand, generally swallow their meals down whole, holding their breath as they do so. So it's thanks to these Permian innovators that we can chew gum without turning blue! Another improvement was having different teeth for different jobs: little front ones for snipping, fangs for ripping, and back teeth for slicing and dicing.

PROCYNOSUCHUS, 2 ft (60 cm) LONG. WE CAN'T KNOW FOR SURE, BUT IT MAY WELL HAVE HAD FUR TO HELP KEEP IT WARM

THAT LADY IS YOUR GREAT-GREAT-GRANDMOTHER, AND THIS FELLOW OVER HERE IS YOUR GREAT-GREAT-GREAT-GREAT-GREAT-GREAT... WELL, YOU GET THE IDEA!

LATE P.M., LATE PERMIAN

It's a peaceful late afternoon 250 million years ago in what is now South Africa. Two *Arctognathus*, big therapsid meat-eaters, are soaking up the last rays of sun on a ledge overlooking a wide floodplain. Several amphibians called *Rhinesuchus* are basking on the sandbars in the river below. On the far bank a herd of *Dicynodon* is browsing among the horsetails. *Glossopteris* grows on the higher spots that don't get flooded too often, and the hilltops are covered in pines.

Nothing in the scene gives any clue as to what's about to happen next…

BEEP!

BEEP!

BEEP!

LADIES AND GENTLEMEN, AN EMERGENCY BROADCAST— A DEVASTATING EXTINCTION IS UNDER WAY. WE HAVE NO WORD YET AS TO THE CAUSE…

WHO KILLED THE PALEOZOIC?

The Paleozoic went out with a bang. At the end of the Permian something wiped out much of life on the planet, and 250 million years later we're still not sure who to blame. Here are some of the suspects:

Suspect A

GIGANTIC AMOUNTS OF LAVA SPEWED OUT OVER SIBERIA RIGHT AROUND THIS TIME. VOLCANIC GASES AND ASH MAY HAVE BEEN THE CULPRITS.

Suspect B

THERE ARE SOME HINTS THAT A COMET OR METEOR MAY HAVE HIT THE EARTH. SCIENTISTS ARE SEARCHING FOR MORE EVIDENCE.

Suspect C

SOME SCIENTISTS THINK ROTTING ORGANIC MATTER PRODUCED POISONOUS GASES THAT GOT TRAPPED UNDER COLD OCEAN WATERS. A CHANGE IN OCEAN TEMPERATURES ALLOWED THE GASES TO SURFACE, KILLING EVERYTHING IN THEIR PATH.

Whatever the cause, the result was that about 90 percent of ocean species and a great number of land plants and animals went extinct in a short amount of time. That's many more species than died in the extinction that put an end to the dinosaurs 185 million years later. Even the insects, which made it through later extinctions with barely a scratch, suffered big losses in this one.

It took the planet a long time to recover. The Triassic started out with dismally low diversity. The few survivors of the big crash multiplied so there were lots of them, but it took a while before they started to branch out into new species. On land, big herds of dicynodonts browsed with little competition. In the ocean there was little reef building, since the creatures that lived attached to the seafloor were some of the hardest hit.

But every end is a new beginning, and in the face of new challenges nature always gets creative. Two groups in particular were in for some big changes. The therapsids, on the one hand, were about to shrink and become true mammals. The archosaurs, on the other hand, were poised to turn into dinosaurs…but that's a whole different story!

The End

APPENDIX I: A TIME LINE OF LIFE ON EARTH

Look! My appendix got taken out!

They don't mean THAT kind, silly!

PRECAMBRIAN

The Earth forms along with the rest of the solar system.

4.5 BILLION YEARS AGO

The Earth is still very hot. It is bombarded by leftover bits and pieces of solar system.

The Earth has cooled. Water vapor rains down for millions of years and fills the oceans.

4 BILLION YEARS AGO

The seawater is loaded with minerals that are the building blocks of big molecules and eventually of life. It is sometimes referred to as the

Primordial Soup

If we traveled this far back, we would die, because the air has no free oxygen in it for us to breathe.

FIRST LIFE!

3.5 BILLION YEARS AGO

Tiny fossils of bacteria (single cells with no nucleus) have been found from this time.

Bacteria called cyanobacteria begin to photosynthesize, meaning they use sunlight to make food. This releases oxygen into the water.

O₂ BURP!

O₂

3 BILLION YEARS AGO

2.5 BILLION YEARS AGO

Cyanobacteria keep pumping oxygen into the oceans. As a result, iron in the seawater rusts and falls to the bottom.

Cyanobacteria form rocky mounds called stromatolites.

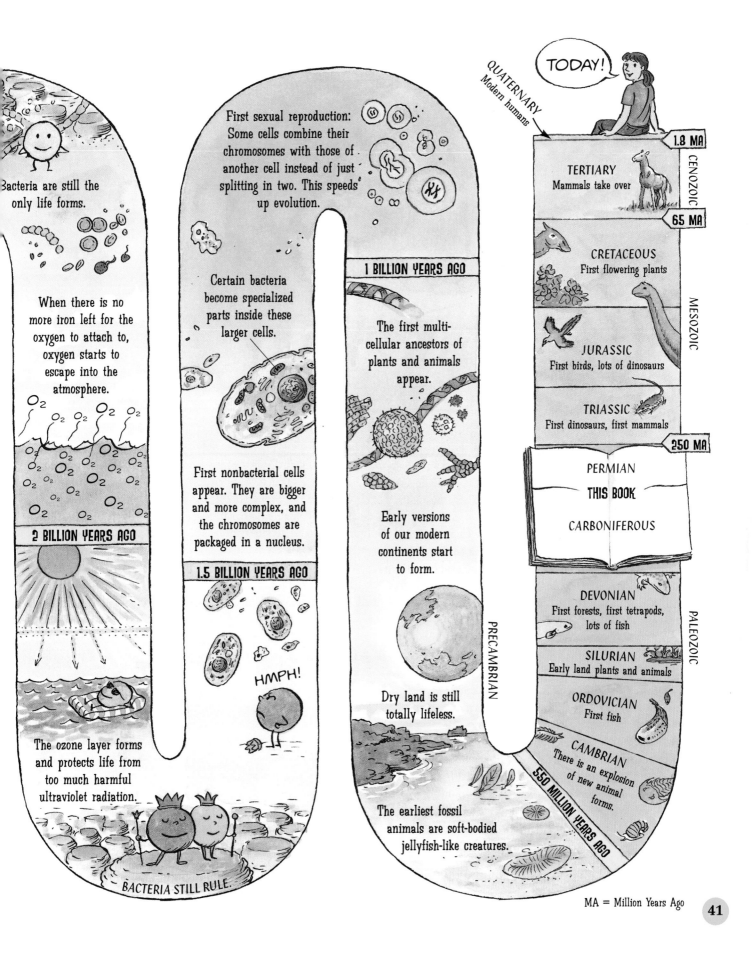

Bacteria are still the only life forms.

When there is no more iron left for the oxygen to attach to, oxygen starts to escape into the atmosphere.

O_2 O_2 O_2 O_2 O_2 O_2 O_2 O_2 O_2 O_2 O_2 O_2 O_2 O_2 O_2 O_2 O_2

2 BILLION YEARS AGO

The ozone layer forms and protects life from too much harmful ultraviolet radiation.

BACTERIA STILL RULE.

First sexual reproduction: Some cells combine their chromosomes with those of another cell instead of just splitting in two. This speeds up evolution.

Certain bacteria become specialized parts inside these larger cells.

First nonbacterial cells appear. They are bigger and more complex, and the chromosomes are packaged in a nucleus.

1.5 BILLION YEARS AGO

HMPH!

1 BILLION YEARS AGO

The first multi-cellular ancestors of plants and animals appear.

Early versions of our modern continents start to form.

Dry land is still totally lifeless.

The earliest fossil animals are soft-bodied jellyfish-like creatures.

PRECAMBRIAN

550 MILLION YEARS AGO

TODAY!

QUATERNARY
Modern humans

1.8 MA

TERTIARY
Mammals take over

CENOZOIC

65 MA

CRETACEOUS
First flowering plants

JURASSIC
First birds, lots of dinosaurs

MESOZOIC

TRIASSIC
First dinosaurs, first mammals

250 MA

PERMIAN

THIS BOOK

CARBONIFEROUS

DEVONIAN
First forests, first tetrapods, lots of fish

SILURIAN
Early land plants and animals

ORDOVICIAN
First fish

CAMBRIAN
There is an explosion of new animal forms.

PALEOZOIC

MA = Million Years Ago

APPENDIX II: A CHART TO HELP KEEP THE VERTEBRATES STRAIGHT

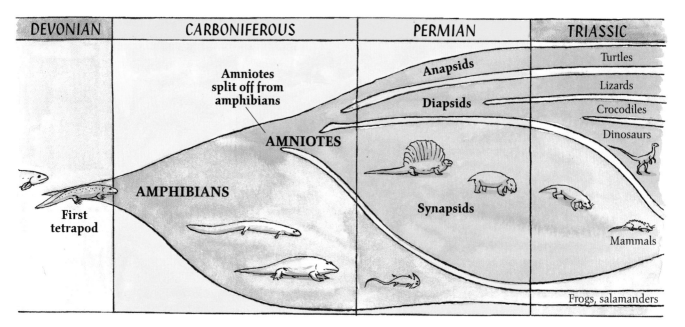

| DEVONIAN | CARBONIFEROUS | PERMIAN | TRIASSIC |

Amniotes split off from amphibians

AMNIOTES

Anapsids

Diapsids

Turtles

Lizards

Crocodiles

Dinosaurs

AMPHIBIANS

First tetrapod

Synapsids

Mammals

Frogs, salamanders

WHERE TO LEARN MORE

The three best places to learn more about the late Paleozoic and its inhabitants are libraries, natural history museums, and the World Wide Web.

If you go to the library, you probably won't find any books just about the Paleozoic, at least not in the children's or young adult section. Luckily, some books about dinosaurs include a chapter or two about what came before. A very nice book that talks about the animals leading up to the dinosaurs is *How Dinosaurs Came to Be,* written by Patricia Lauber and illustrated by Douglas Henderson (Simon and Schuster). Books like the DK/American Museum of Natural History's *Dinosaur Encyclopedia* and the *Simon and Schuster Encyclopedia of Dinosaurs and Other Prehistoric Creatures* include quite a few Carboniferous and Permian animals. Books about the evolution of life also cover this period.

It's also worth checking out the adult section. Two very good books of this sort that are not directed specifically at children but are full of pictures and readable in-depth information are *Prehistoric Journey,* by Kirk Johnson and Richard Stucky (Denver Museum of Natural History) and *Prehistoric Life,* by David Norman (Macmillan).

My favorite thing to do on the Web is to use the Google image search. You go to www.google.com and click on Images. Then type in a name — for example, "Scutosaurus" — and

presto! — lots of pictures of this ungainly animal and its fossil bones appear. Only the most obscure life-forms won't get you any hits. Always remember that not everything you come across as you browse the Web is accurate, since anyone can set up a Web page, whether they are knowledgeable or not. If you need to find detailed information about a particular period or creature, you can try www.palaeos.com. It's not for the faint of heart — it's full of scientific terms — but it's also chock-full of hard-to-find information. An interesting site about insects, Roy Beckmeyer's www.windsofkansas.com/fossil_insects.html, has a link to wonderful reconstructions of dragonflies and other invertebrates by the German Werner Kraus. For maps of the prehistoric world, try www.scotese.com, click on Earth History, and then choose a time period.

I'm afraid I have given aquatic life only two pages when it could easily fill a whole book. One of the interesting creatures I left out for lack of space is the Tully Monster, the state fossil of Illinois. You can check out this most improbable creature at http://www.museum.state.il.us/exhibits/symbols/fossil.html.

The Web ties in with the other great resource, natural history museums. If you aren't lucky enough to live near one, you can consult their web sites to find out what's in them. Some of the museum sites, such as that of the Berkeley Museum of Natural History (www.ucmp.berkeley.edu), include a lot of extra information and can also be a good source if you are writing a report or simply want to learn more.

Best of all, of course, is actually visiting a museum. The Denver Museum of Natural History has a particularly nice diorama of a late Carboniferous scene, for example. The National Museum of Natural History in Washington, D.C. (check out a fairly small diorama of a coal swamp with a giant dragonfly in its Insect Zoo), the American Museum of Natural History in New York, and many other museums both large and small have exhibits about Paleozoic life.

ACKNOWLEDGMENTS

I would like to thank the four reviewers who kindly shared their knowledge with me and prevented me from making all sorts of mistakes. Any remaining mistakes are mine alone.

William A. DiMichele, Curator of Fossil Plants at the Smithsonian Institution, guided me through the plants and helped me understand what a coal swamp really looked like.

Cary Easterday, graduate student at Ohio State University and co-discoverer of the world's largest fossil cockroach, advised me on invertebrates.

Corwin Sullivan, a graduate student and teaching fellow at Harvard, took time from studying dinosaur anklebones to check on my vertebrates and to tell me about wonderful creatures I hadn't heard of, such as the burrowing dicynodont *Diictodon*.

John Beck, a researcher at the Weston Observatory of Boston College, made sure I got the geology right.

I am grateful to the following paleontologists whom I consulted, either via e-mail or in person:

Simon Braddy, University of Bristol, United Kingdom

Robert Carroll, Redpath Museum, McGill University, Canada

Karen Chin, University of Colorado at Boulder, Colorado

Jason Dunlop, Museum für Naturkunde der Humboldt-Universität, Berlin, Germany

Kirk Johnson, Denver Museum of Natural History, Colorado

Jozef Klembara, Comenius University, Slovak Republic

Andrew Knoll, Harvard University, Cambridge, Massachusetts

Conrad Labandeira, National Museum of Natural History, Smithsonian Institution, Washington, D.C.

Warm thanks also to many others who helped in a variety of ways, including Josep Antoni Alcover, Bruce Archibald, Anthony Bonner, John Bonner, Amy Davidson, Nik Mills, Mary Parrish, and Stephen Priestley. Marcia Ciro did the final design of the book, which took both creativity and patience. As for my family and friends, I couldn't have done it without them.

Most of all I want to thank my editor, Nancy Laties Feresten, for realizing how very cool (and seriously underrepresented) the late Paleozoic is, and for asking me to do a book about it.

AUTHOR'S SOURCES FOR TEXT AND IMAGES

BOOKS:

Caroll, Robert L. *Vertebrate Paleontology and Evolution.* New York: W.H. Freeman and Co., 1988

Czerkas, Sylvia J. and Stephen A. Czerkas. *Dinosaurs, A Global View.* New York: Mallard Press, 1991

Dingus, Lowell, et al. *Mammals and their Extinct Relatives: A Guide to the Lila Acheson Wing.* New York: American Museum of Natural History, 1994

Fortey, Richard. *Life, A Natural History of the First Four Billion Years of Life on Earth.* Vintage Books, 1999

Gould, Stephen J., ed. *The Book of Life: An Illustrated History of the Evolution of Life on Earth.* New York: W.W. Norton and Co., 1993

Johnson, Kirk R. and Richard K. Stuckey. *Prehistoric Journey, A History of Life on Earth.* Boulder: Denver Museum of Natural History/Roberts Rinehart Publishers, 1995

Lauber, Patricia and Douglas Henderson. *How Dinosaurs Came to Be.* New York: Simon and Schuster Books for Young Readers, 1996

Maisey, John G. et al. *The Hall of Vertebrate Origins: A Guide to Fishes, Amphibians, Turtles, Lizards, Crocodiles, and Pterosaurs.* New York: American Museum of Natural History, 1996

McKerrow, W.S., ed. *The Ecology of Fossils.* Cambridge: MIT Press, 1979

McLoughlin, John C. *Synapsida: A New Look at the Origin of Mammals.* New York: Viking Press, 1980

Norman, David. *Prehistoric Life: The Rise of Vertebrates.* New York: Macmillan, 1994

Palmer, Douglas, Ed. *The Simon and Schuster Encyclopedia of Dinosaurs and Prehistoric Creatures.* New York: Simon and Schuster, 1999

Piveteau, Jean, Directeur. *Traité de Paléontologie,* Vol. 3. Paris: Masson, 1953-1961

Priestley, Stephen. *Hot Blood: The Emergence of Mammals, parts I and II.* Gibsons, B.C.: icon words&images, 1999

Quicke and Rasnitsyn. *History of Insects.* Boston: Kluwer Academic, 2001

Ross, H.H. *A Textbook of Entomology,* 2nd ed. New York: Wiley, 1948

Stewart, W.N. & G.W. Rothwell.: *Paleobotany and the Evolution of Plants,* 2nd ed. Cambridge: Cambridge University Press, 1993

Wood, Rachel. *Reef Evolution.* Oxford: Oxford University Press,1999

ARTICLES:

Braddy, S.J. and D.E.G. Briggs. 2002. "New Lower Permian Nonmarine Arthropod Trace Fossils from New Mexico and South Africa." *Journal of Paleontology,* 76 (3546-554)

Brauckmann, C. and W. Zessin. 1989. "Neue Meganeuridae aur dem Namurian von Hagen-Vorhalle (BRD) und die Phylogenie der Meganisoptera (Insecta, Odonata)." *Deutsche Entomologische Zeitschrift,* N.F. 36(1/3): 177-215

Coates, M.I. and S.E.K. Sequeira. 2001. "A New Stethacanthid Chondrichthyan from the Lower Carboniferous of Beardsden, Scotland." *Journal of Vertebrate Paleontology,* 21(3):438-459

DiMichele,W.A. and T. L. Phillips. 1994. "Paleobotanical and paleoecological constraints on peat formation in the late Carboniferous of Euramerica." *Palaeogeography, Palaeoclimatology, Palaeoecology,* 106: 39-90

DiMichele,W.A. and J.W. Nelson. 1989. "Small-Scale Spatial Heterogeneity in Pennsylvanian-Age Vegetation from the Roof Shale of the Springfield Coal (Illinois Basin)." *Palaios,* 4:276-280

Dunlop, J.A. 1995. "Gigantism in Arthropods." *Forum of the American Tarantula Society,* 4(5): 145-147

Gastaldo, R.A., H.W. Pfefferkorn, and W.A. DiMichele. 1996. "Out of the Icehouse and into the Greenhouse: A Late Paleozoic Analog for Modern Global Vegetational Change." *GSA Today,* 6, (10): 1-7

Hünicken, M. 1980. "A Giant Fossil Spider (Megarachne servinei) from Bajo de Véliz, Upper Carboniferous, Argentina." *Boletín de la Academia Nacional de Ciencias (Argentina),* 53 (3/4): 317-325

Jeram, A.J. 1994. "Scorpions from the Viséan of East Kirkton, West Lothian, Scotland, with a revision of the infraorder Mesoscorpionina." *Transactions of the Royal Society of Edinburgh: Earth Sciences,* 84: 283-299

Kerr, R.A. 2001. "Whiff of Gas Points to Impact Mass Extinction." *Science,* February 2001. 291: 1469-1470

Klembara, J. and S. Mesaros. 1992. "New Finds of Discosauriscus Austiracus (Makowsky 1876) from the Lower Permian of Boskovice Furrow (Czecho-Slovakia)." *Geologica Carpathica,* 45 (5): 305-312

Phillips, T. L. and W.A. DiMichele. 1992. "Comparative Ecology and Life –History and Biology of Arborescent Lycopsids in Late Carboniferous Swamps of Euramerica." *Annals of the Missouri Botanical Garden,* 79: 560-588

THE WEB:

Many web sites were helpful in researching this book. A tiny sample:

White, T., et al. "Paleos: The Trace of Life on Earth." Available online at www.palaeos.com.

Beckmeyer, R. "Fossil Insects." Available online at www.windsofkansas.com/fossil_insects.html.

"The Tree of Life Web Project." Available online at http://tolweb.org.

Scotese, P. "Paleomap Project." Available online at www.scotese.com.

Index

One of the world's largest nonprofit scientific and educational organizations, the National Geographic Society was founded in 1888 "for the increase and diffusion of geographic knowledge." Fulfilling this mission, the Society educates and inspires millions every day through its magazines, books, television programs, videos, maps and atlases, research grants, the National Geographic Bee, teacher workshops, and innovative classroom materials. The Society is supported through membership dues, charitable gifts, and income from the sale of its educational products. This support is vital to National Geographic's mission to increase global understanding and promote conservation of our planet through exploration, research, and education.

For more information, please call 1-800-NGS LINE (647-5463) or write to the following address:
NATIONAL GEOGRAPHIC SOCIETY
1145 17th Street N.W.
Washington, D.C. 20036-4688 U.S.A.
Visit the Society's Web site at www.nationalgeographic.com.

Book design by Hannah Bonner and Marcia Ciro
The text is set in Gilgamesh medium.

Library of Congress Cataloging-in-Publication Data available on request.

ISBN 0-7922-6326-X

Printed in Belgium

How to pronounce the scientific names in this book

Akmonistion (ak-mon-ISS-tee-on)
Archeopteryx (AR-kee-OP-ter-iks)
Archosaurus (AR-ko-SORE-us)
Arctognathus (ark-tug-NATH-us)
Arthropleura (AR-thro-PLUR-uh)
Autunia (aw-TOO-nee-uh)
blastoids (BLAS-toids)
brachiopods (BRAK-ee-oh-pods)
bryozoans (bri-oh-ZOW-ans)
Cacops (KAY-kops)
Cambrian (KAM-bree-an)
Carboniferous (KAR-bo-NI-fur-us)
caseid (KAY-see-id)
Cenozoic (sen-oh-ZO-ic)
Coelurosauravus (see-lur-oh-sawr-AV-us)
Cotylorhynchus (ko-TILE-oh-RINK-us)
Crassigyrinus (crass-ih-jur-EYE-nus)
Cretaceous (kree-TAY-she-us)
crinoids (KRY-noids)
Devonian (de-VOW-nee-an)
Diaphorodendron
  (die-AF-or-oh-DEN-dron)
ciapsid (die-AP-sid)
cicynodont (die-SY-no-dahnt)
Diictodon (die-IK-toe-DON)
Dimetrodon (die-MEE-tro-don)
Diplocaulus (dip-low-CAW-luss)
Discosauriscus (dis-co-sawr-ISS-cus)
Dolichosoma (doe-lick-oh-SO-ma)
Edaphosaurus (eh-DAFF-oh-SAWR-us)

Eocaptorhinus (ee-oh-cap-ter-HI-nus)
Eryops (AIR-ee-ops)
eurypterid (yer-IP-ter-id)
fusulinids (FEW-su-LINE-ids)
Glossopteris (gloss-OP-ter-iss)
Gondwana (gon-DWON-ah)
Greererpeton (greer-AIR-pet-on)
Haptodus (hap-TOE-dus)
Hibbertopterus (hib-er-TOP-ter-us)
Hovasaurus (hov-a-SAWR-us)
Hylonomus (hi-lo-NO-mus)
Janassa (ja-NASS-ah)
Jurassic (je-RASS-ic)
Limnoscelis (lim-NOSS-e-liss)
Lycaenops (lie-SEEN-ops)
lycopod (LIE-co-pod)
Meganeuropsis permiana
  (MEG-ah-ner-OP-sis per-mee-AN-uh)
Megarachne (meg-uh-RAK-nee)
Mesozoic (meh-zuh-ZO-ic)
Mississippian (miss-ih-SIP-ee-an)
monurans (mo-NUR-ans)
Moschops (MOSS-kops)
nautiloids (NAWT-uh-loids)
Ophiacodon (oh-fee-AH-ko-don)
Ordovician (or-do-VISH-ee-an)
Orthacanthus (or-tha-KAN-thus)
palaeodictyopteran
  (pay-lee-oh-dick-tee-OP-ter-an)
Paleozoic (pay-lee-oh-ZOH-ik)

Paliguana (pa-lig-WAN-uh)
Pangaea (pan-JEE-uh)
Panthalassa (pan-thal-AH-suh)
Pantylus (pan-TIE-lus)
Paralycopodites
  (pa-ra-lie-koh-po-DIE-tees)
pareiasaur (per-EYE-ah-sawr)
Pelycosaurs (PEL-ih-koh-sawrs)
Pennsylvanian (pen-sil-VAY-nee-an)
Permian (PURR-mee-an)
Petrolacosaurus
  (pet-roh-lack-oh-SAWR-us)
Procynosuchus (pro-sy-no-SOOK-us)
Protorosaurus (pro-to-ro-SAWR-us)
Pulmonoscorpius
  (pul-moh-no-SCOR-pee-us)
Quaternary (KWA-ter-nair-ee)
Rhinesuchus (rie-ne-SOOK-us)
Scutosaurus (skoo-ta-SAWR-us)
Sigillaria (si-jill-AHR-ee-ah)
Silurian (si-LU-ree-an)
synapsid (sin-AP-sid)
Synchysidendron (sin-kie-si-DEN-dron)
Tertiary (TER-shee-air-ee)
Tethys Sea (TETH-iss see)
therapsids (theh-RAP-sids)
Triassic (try-ASS-ik)
Tuditanus (too-di-TAN-us)
Varanosaurus (va-ran-oh-SAWR-us)
Xenacanthus (zee-na-KAN-thus)

Glossary of words not defined in the text

Arachnids: A group of invertebrate animals that includes spiders, scorpions, ticks, and mites.
Bugs: In this book, bug is used in the popular sense that includes insects and other terrestrial invertebrates such as spiders, centipedes, worms, and the like.
Cannibalism: The act of eating a member of one's own species.
Carnivorous: An adjective that describes an animal that eats other animals (plants that eat animals are carnivorous as well).
Chromosomes: Strands of protein containing information for making a new cell.
Delta: A broad marshy area created by a river as it flows out to the sea.

Embryo: The early stage of development of an animal before it is born or hatched. Plants that are still inside the seed are also called embryos.
Fossil: Remains or traces of a living being that over millions of years have turned into stone.
Invertebrate: An animal without a backbone.
Niche: A set of opportunities to live that a species makes use of within its environment. For example, one plant may be well designed to live in a warm wet place with some shade; another plant may be better at living in a dry sunny place.

Nucleus: A little rounded bag inside most cells which contains chromosomes.
Nymph: An immature insect, a nymph is similar to a larva, but looking more like the adult animal. Dragonflies and cockroaches start out as nymphs.
Ozone layer: A layer of ozone (O3, a form of oxygen with a strong odor) surrounding the earth 10—20 miles above its surface.
Temperate: Describes a climate that is moderate—neither very hot nor very cold.
Ultraviolet radiation: Also known as UV light, it is a form of light that we can't see, but which causes sunburn.
Vertebrate: An animal with a backbone.